Best Christmas Book For Kids

Introduction

Christmas tops the list of favorite holidays for many children. In fact, some would say that youngsters base their entire year around

Christmas. children have even been proverbial to start out pondering what they need for Christmas as early as January! however, there's far more to Christmas than simply gifts. Christmas could be a time for family in any case, love, similarly as tradition. Keep reading if you wish to seek out amazing Christmas facts for kids!

Christmas question and answers for kids!

THE HISTORY OF CHRISTMAS DAY

Christmas celebrates the day that Jesus was born to Joseph and The Virgin MARY within the megacity of Bethlehem. The New Testament teaches that Jesus Christ is that the Son of God and came to Earth as a person to die for our sins. AN innocent man, he was crucified around thirty three times late. Jesus Christ was additionally buried in a very grave, however once 3 days he rose once more and mounted into heaven.

No one is bound specifically what day Jesus Christ was born. There ar some hints, still, within the

Gospel of Luke that time to Jesus' birth within the month of December. It's allowed

that initial the primary fests were on January sixth and also the first citation of December twenty fifth is in a very handwriting from the time 354.

Celebrating Christmas failed to return an oversized event within the us till the center of the 1800s. concerning this point, the day began to return a preferred time for family gatherings. In 1870 the day came a sanctioned civil vacation within the North American country and has adult additional well-liked since.

CHRISTMAS QUESTION AND ANSWERS

What does Christmas Day celebrate?

Christmas Day praises the introduction of Jesus Christ.

When is Christmas celebrated?

Christmas is praised on December 25th

Who commends this day?

This day is a Christian excursion celebrated by Christians all over the planet. Various non-Christians likewise praise this day as a period of harmony, happiness, family, and giving of presents.

How truly do individuals celebrate?

There are heaps of ways that individuals observe Christmas. most extreme individuals get along with family and trade presents on Christmas morning. various individuals go to chapel gatherings either on Christmas Day or Christmas Eve.

Christmas beautifications are a major piece of the get-away. Individuals adorn their homes with happy lights and free time enrichments. They likewise for the most part set up a Christmas tree and decorate it with beautifiers and lights.

One more piece of the merriment of Christmas will be Christmas melodies comparable as Quiet

Evening, Down in a Trough, The Main Noel, The Twelve Days of Christmas, and Signal Ringers.

In the US Christmas is a public common excursion. most extreme taxpayer supported organizations, theological schools, and business are shut for Christmas.

For what reason do we observe Christmas?

Christmas is the party of the introduction of Jesus.

When did Christmas come a common excursion in the US?

Christmas came a common excursion in 1870

What are some Christmas customs?

Having a Christmas tree, finishing your home with Christmas lights, burning get-away eyefuls, singing Christmas chorales, moving Christmas cards, investing energy with musketeers and family.

What does the X depend on in X-Mas?

X is the image for Christ in Greek. once in a while individuals utilize the X to dock the word Christmas and simply relate it to X-Mas.

What's the significance here for youngsters?

CHRISTMAS MEANS to give and to concede presents. It

likewise means to observe Jesus' introduction to the world and to rejoin with relatives. What's more, just to make the day's end fancier, you have a major banquet. Another practice is to adorn the Christmas tree with varicolored lights

FUN FACTS ABOUT CHRISTMAS

- If you add up all the gifts given within the song the Twelve Days of Christmas, there are 364 total gifts.
- The American state to acknowledge

Christmas has holidays was Alabama. OK was the last state to try to to therefore.

- The tradition of the Christmas tree comes from the country of Federal Republic of Germany. The earliest proverbial decorations for the tree were apples.

- The 1st North American country postage with a Christian theme was in 1962.
- Around 1/6 of all retail sales within the

us are Christmas purchases.

HAPPY CHRISTMAS IN DIFFERENT LANGUAGES

Kids, Christmas is upon us!

Do you want to stand out from your friends at Christmas and New Year's Eve parties? For their benefit, how about we speak various languages from various continents? Let's demonstrate your proficiency in foreign languages

- French: Joyeux Noël
- German: Frohe Weinachten
- Spanish: Feliz Navidad
- Italian: Buon Natale
- Portuguese: Feliz Natal

- Dutch: Vrolijk kerstfeest
- Romanian: Crăciun fericit
- Polish: Wesołych świąt Bożego Narodzenia
- Swedish: God Jul
- Czech: Veselé Vánoc

HISTORY OF SANTA CLAUS 1

1-Once upon a time in the North Pole, Santa Claus lived in a cozy cottage with his wife Mrs. Claus and a team of elves who helped him prepare for Christmas. Every year, Santa would make a list of all the good boys and girls around the world and check it twice to see who had been naughty or nice. On Christmas Eve, he would pack his sleigh with presents and set off on his magical journey, delivering gifts to all the deserving children. But one year, Santa was feeling particularly exhausted and overwhelmed. The list of good children seemed to grow longer each year and he wasn't sure if he could make it to every house in time. Mrs. Claus, noticing her husband's distress, came up with a plan. She gathered all the elves and together they created a special device that could help Santa deliver presents faster and more efficiently. On Christmas Eve, Santa loaded up his sleigh with the presents and the new device, and set off on his journey. And to his amazement, the device worked perfectly,

HISTORY OF SANTA CLAUS 2

Once upon a time, in a land far, far away, there lived a kind and jolly old man named Santa Claus. Santa was known for his love of children and his passion for spreading joy and happiness wherever he went. He lived in a cozy little cottage at the North Pole, surrounded by his trusty team of elves who helped him make toys all year round. On the night before Christmas, Santa would pack his sleigh with toys and set off on his journey around the world, delivering presents to all the good boys and girls. He would travel far and wide, using his magical sleigh and eight reindeer to guide him through the snowy skies. Despite the cold and snowy weather, Santa always had a warm smile on his face and a twinkle in his eye. He loved nothing more than seeing the joy on the faces of the children when they woke up on Christmas morning and found their presents under the tree. As the years went by, Santa's legend grew and he became known as the bringer of joy and happiness at Christmas time.

?

www.ingramcontent.com/pod-product-compliance
Lightning Source LLC
LaVergne TN
LVHW020527160826
845677LV00015B/3945
* 9 7 9 8 3 6 9 8 7 1 3 3 1 *